A Collection of Inspirational
& Motivational, Poems, Prayers,
Spiritual Messages, & More

Mesha D.

Jesus has endorsed this book.

Printed in the United States
Documented by the Library of Congress
ISBN # 0-615-11874-7
First Edition

Cover Page and Sketches Thought of By:
Yours Truly, Mesha D.

Note: This book gives NO CREDIT to the adversary, serpent, devil, and / or enemy.

HE Create Publishing™

A Brief Glance About the Writer

Mesha is a 31 year young Southerner, who started writing as a hobby. Her writing skills increased with education, experiences, excitements, disappointments, pick ups, & let downs. She has been allotted recognition strictly from Heaven.

Today, Ms. Wallace is connecting with people to spread her talent, as Jesus word was spread over a thousand cattle. Psalms 50:10

From The Sentiments Of My Heart, embodies art and words, that rest in the depth of the writer's heart. This young aspiring woman is looking to Jesus for her needs according to His existing riches in Glory.

Contents

Special Thanks

First and far most important, I would like to Thank, the Seed, Root & Offspring, my Lord and Personal Savior Jesus Christ for all the many Blessings that He has stored upon me through His Word and Power of the Holy Spirit. Second, the roots, Mr. & Mrs. James E. are recognized as two special people in my life. Thank You mom & dad. Jeanette, James, Hazel, my nieces and nephews, the flower peddles, Thank You for the love and support that you display during my continual walks of life. These include the good, the bad, and the in between.

Special Thanks continue to go out to my Inspirations, Motivations, and Power Plants. These include:

Jesus Christ

Eld. Jesse Alston Family
Sis. Patricia Archer
Jean Baker
David L. Bowen Family
Melba Boyd
Mssnry Katherine Braswell
Endtime Church Family
Mnstr Melvin Davis
Linda Dunston
Eason Family
Mable Hargrove Family
Francis Harper
Sylvester Harrison Family
William Harrison, Jr. Family
William Harrison, Sr (deceased)
Tommie Hewitt, Sr. Family
Ida (Grandma—deceased)
Dr. Mary Kimble
Bishop Joseph King, Sr. Family
John T. Knight Family
Tony Lynch
Pastor Hope Lyons
Marbet Family
Pastor & 1st Lady W. McNair
Aunt Rosa Noel
Chandra Owens
Ronnie Parker
Janice Perry
Pauline (Grandma—deceased)
Dr. Norma Ragland
John Richardson Family
Katherine Roberts
Barbara Saulsberry
Cornelius Strickland (deceased)
Major Benie Umstead
Mr. Larry Waddell
Richard Williams
Mssnry Mamie Worrell

Special Thanks go to a few others, who are special in my heart, that I did not list by name. You influenced the spark in my fire, to keep pressing on, to the Mark of the High Calling, which is in Christ Jesus.

Message from the Writer

I am honored to know, Jesus chose me, from among the many sheep of His people to be used, to glorify Him. To all of the listener's under the sound of my voice, in writing, I would like to extend a sincere Thank You. Your support has motivated me, to go forth & be used more by God. When you steal away time with this book, I believe that you will receive a refreshing within your Spirit Man. I pray that you will be continuously Blessed. For those who are True Worshiper's and Sincere Prayer Worriers, pray my strength in the Lord. 2 Thess 1:11-12 For the babes in Christ, keep on seeking the Lord, while He may be found, by developing a personal relationship with Him. Isaiah 55:6-9 This includes talking with God and making confessions and asking Him for perfection, in your understanding this Spiritual Journey.

Take ownership of your investment and treasure the art and words close at heart.

This book is a Blessing to anyone with a Jesus Partaking Spirit.

About the Book

This book has been in the developmental phase since year 1994. Unaware of the creation of a book, Mesha began writing poetry as a hobby. When a thought presented itself, she would make note of it. Mesha continued to write, only to look back and discover, the birthing of a Blessing.

After reviewing a few gospel taped services, and peaking back at some of her life's experiences, she realized poetry, inspirations, motivations, spiritual messages, & more were Heaven sent, from Author Jesus.

This book embodies art and word that reflects the heart felt moments of what the writer was thinking; observations of what she have seen, has heard, experienced or experiencing. It is designed to allow the reader to become a partaker, while relating to personal experiences.

Mesha has encamped heart felt experiences during the tests of time, while weathering the storms that blew her way. The messages enclosed within this book put enemies to shame, as Jesus place them at her feet. Hebrew 1:13

Before reading this book, say a prayer for comfort, while placing your mind at a spiritual plateau, to receive what Jesus has created through such a Blessed, Holy, & Aspiring young woman. After having read this book, Thank God for the many Blessings that He has stored upon you, through your Birthing Power.

Listening Audience, please pay close attention to the words and how you can relate your personal experiences. Allow Jesus to talk with you during your moments of seeking inspiration & motivation, as you enjoy this Heaven sent book.

Thank You Jesus

Dear Jesus:

I have come, to Thank You for being Faithful and Just in all things. As I grow to understand, there are no set times to give Thanks. Each day I awake out of my unconscious sleep is an opportunity to give Thanks unto You. As I continue to give Thanks to You, *The Blessing*, there are extended blessings that follow Your provision of Self. Because I am so overwhelmed with wanting to Thank You, *Jesus*, I will pattern after David.

He gave Thanks to You in song. Pslms 28:7 He gave Thanks for Your name being near. Pslms 75:1 He gave Thanks because You give us the victory. Pslms 60:12 He gave Thanks because You are good. Pslms 107:1 David said, "I will give Thanks forever." Pslms 30:12 Not to neglect Timothy, he gave Thanks to You in all things. 1 Timothy

Paul said, "Now thanks be to God who always leads us in triumph in Christ, and through us diffuses the fragrance of His knowledge in every place. For we are to God the fragrance of Christ among those who are being saved and among those who are perishing." 2Corinthians 2:13&14 Paul continued by saying, "Rejoice in the Lord always. Again I will say, rejoice! Let your gentleness be known to all men. The Lord is at hand. Be anxious for nothing, but in everything by prayer and supplication, with thanksgiving, let your request be made known unto God; and the peace of God, which surpasses all understanding, will guard your hearts and minds through Christ Jesus." Philippians 4:4-7

I will continue to come before You, *Jesus*, with Thanksgiving; whether at the dinner table; driving a vehicle; sitting in silence; on my knee's; or in the presence of men & women. I am reminded to enter Your gates with thanksgiving, and into Your courts with Praise. Psalms 100:4 My Praises will accent the Prayer's set before Your Throne. I will be thankful unto You and bless Your Name. I will be so humble, as to Honor and Adore You, for I know that Your Grace and Mercy is Sufficient. 2Cor12:9

Thank You Jesus For Everything!

POWER

Walking With God

Makes You

POWERFUL!

Not
Popular

1 Colossians 1:11&12

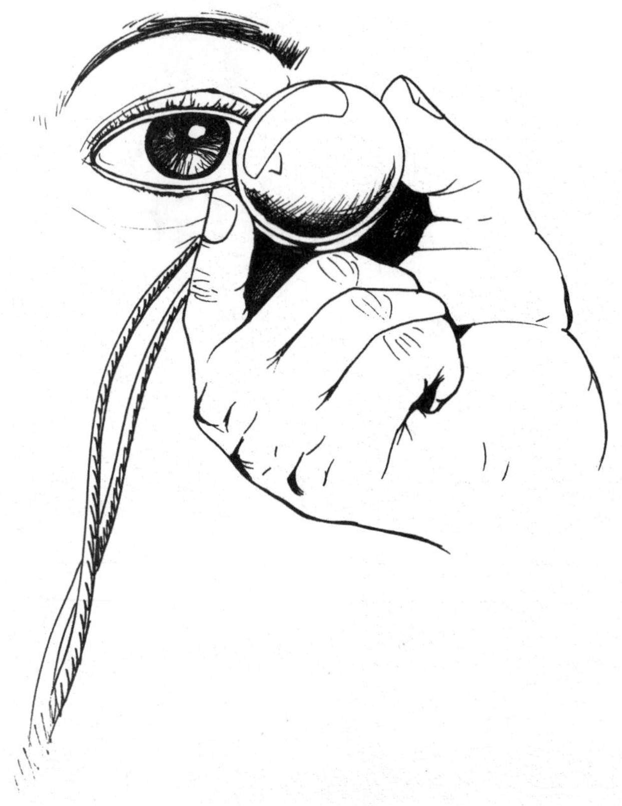

LOOKING FROM THE MICRO GLASS

The lens, the lens
The lens is so small it blocks my view
I see an image of a person, the question asked Is Who

I'm not looking through a mirror
I'm looking through a reflecting glass
Hoping that the bleary shadow will soon clear & pass

Every time I look
I see something white as snow
Whenever I travel, the image is everywhere I go

Because the micro glass is so small
I can only look in with one eyeball

But I constantly peak to see who I see
The image of this vessel not being me

Sometimes I look so hard, the view grabs my eye
Holding it tight making me appear to be a spy

The micro glass is an unusual tool
If you don't look careful, you may get fooled

One day I decided to question the image that I saw
Who are you in the unclear view?

Surprising to hear a strong sound of mind
A male voice spoke, I Am The Image About To Make Them Blind

Then I realized, it was the Holy Spirit making it difficult to see
Reflecting back to the inside of me

I Praise God, for taking my eyes to another spiritual level
Being honored to know the image I saw was He & not the devil

Jesus continued the conversation to say
Everywhere you travel, I've paved the way

I may appear small and bleary as can be
Looking from the micro glass is the eye unlocking key

Everything, everything, that you see
Was placed by God coming directly from me
    1 Corinthians 13:9 - 13
    2 Corinthians 13:5 & 6

Personal Testimony

FOR THE MAKING

STIR ME

RIP ME

BUILD ME

MAKE ME COMPLETE

Psalms 19:7

Spiritual Food to support your daily maturity in Christ

LEARNING

As We Live
We Learn It

A wise man will hear and increase learning,
And a man of understanding will attain wise counsel
Proverbs 1:5

Live By The Word In Your Home

Your house is not a home without the word and the living
Jesus paid the price and we must start giving *Genesis 42:18*

You may ask, "What does this really mean?"
The word answers, "Jesus is Lord of Lord and
King of Kings" *1 Timothy 6:15*

It doesn't take much to find what we need for a home
God said, He will supply all of our needs *Isaiah 58:11*

Ask, and it will be given to you
Seek, and you will find *Matthew 7:7*

Knock, and it will be opened to you
All of this is in The Word *Matthew 7:7*

God's word tells us that we must be saved, sanctified
And filled with the Holy Spirit *1 Corinthians 6*

When this has taken place in our lives
We have applied the word to our living *Genesis 3:22*

By placing God's word to action in our lives
We live in spiritual homes and not ungodly houses
Joshua 2:18

HOLY SPIRIT

GUIDED BY THE HOLY SPIRIT

Guided by The Holy Spirit
to be so strong in God's word
that nothing or no one can shake my faith. James 2:10

Guided by The Holy Spirit
that where Jesus leads, I will follow. Deuteronomy 16:20

Guided by The Holy Spirit
to be an example as a Christian. 1 Peter 4:16

Guided by The Holy Spirit
that the Lord will always remain my Shepherd.
David said, "The Lord is my Shepherd." Psalms 23:1

Guided by The Holy Spirit
to obey God's word for "the wages of sin is death
but the gift of God is eternal life through Christ Jesus our
Lord." Romans 6:23

Guided by The Holy Spirit
to honor God's doctrine for Jeremiah prayed,
"Ah Lord God you have made the heavens and the
earth with your great power and outstretched arm. There is
nothing too hard for You." Jeremiah 32:17

Guided by The Holy Spirit
to continue my walk in Holiness, Jesus
instructed Moses to tell the children of Israel, they shall be
Holy, " for I am the Lord Your God Am Holy."
Leviticus 19:2

Are you ready to be guided by The Holy Spirit?

HEAVEN

It's the most sacred place that ones soul could possibly live. It is not compared to any other reachable place. It has a floor plan that will never allow your feet to get dirty. It is a protection. We don't have to worry about pollution, the ozone layer, the temperature, it's height, or it's depth. We must constantly work towards the mark of the high calling, which is found in Christ Jesus. *Philippians 3* Heaven has this gravitational pull, that only draws the Righteous Soul. *Revelation 3:21*

One may ask, "Why is this place so constantly talked about but very few actions are shown from the pulpit to home?" The answer is quite obvious. Jesus and all of His Heavenly Ordinances reside here. Heaven is Gods' house, designed especially for the righteous soul's of mankind. In order to reach this place called Heaven, we must follow the instructions. However, many want to be hear's and not doer's of God's word. *Psalms 95*

There are many assemblies or churches, who are full of flesh family and not enough Spiritual family. The word church is not to be taken lightly. Everyone who assemble themselves with other worshiper's is not the church. Those who do the will of the Father is the True Church. Paul stated, "that He might present it to Himself a glorious church, not having spot or wrinkle or any such thing, but that it should be holy without blemish. Ephesians 5:27 Jesus made it as plain as day in *Mark Chapter 3 verse 35*, "For whosoever shall do the will of God, the same is my brother, and my sister, and mother."

Observing individual everyday lives, we don't spend enough time practicing holy behavior. Holy & Heaven are a pair. As we understand Heaven, we must note that our actions should model holiness in our walk, talk, attitude, and appearance.

While living on earth, we are to adopt the like mind of Jesus Christ and His Righteousness. Just as He stated in His word, "Most assuredly, I say to you, he who believes in Me, the works that I do he will do also; and greater works than these he will do, because I go to My Father." *John 14:12* This passage was written for you and I. These works are yet to be performed and seen by men. It is believed by Holy men & women of God, THIS TO SHALL COME TO PASS.

We must perform Holy behavior, for our souls to receive a Heavenly resting place. True saints of God, who are Heaven bound are few and far between. God made the path to this place called Heaven, straight and narrow. *Matthew 7:14* God's word provides a beautiful description of Heaven and He was so kind, as to provide a road map for the journey. If we take our time, while reading the word, without rushing through the living instructions and Obey; it is *"Holy Word Guaranteed"* that our souls will arrive in *Heaven.*

Acts 7:49&50

For Best Results, Read The Book.....

Genesis through Revelation

AMEN

If You Have Followed God's Orders

Throughout This Work Day

Practicing Obedience Is Better

Than Sacrifice, Just Say:

AMEN

For Your Work Day Has Just Been Made Complete.

Refer to the book of Romans

Lord, Lift Us Up Where We Belong

If our eyes have not seen and ears have not heard
Lord, Lift Us Up Where We Belong *1 Corinthians 2:9*

If the words of our mouth and the meditation of our hearts
have not been acceptable within thy sight
Lord, Lift Us Up Where We Belong *Psalms 19:14*

If we have not been walking in the path of righteousness
for Your Name Sake
Lord, Lift Us Up Where We Belong *Psalms 23:3*

If we have fallen short in treating our family
and neighbor's right
Lord, Lift Us Up Where We Belong *Hosea 14:9*

If our faith have not been the substance of
things hoped for,
evidence in things not seen
Lord, Lift Us Up Where We Belong *Hebrew 11:1*

If we have lacked in knowing that Peace surpasses
all understanding
Lord, Lift Us Up Where We Belong *Philippians 4:7*

If we have not acknowledged You in all of our ways
For the asking, Dear Lord, Lift Us Up Where We Belong
Deuteronomy 10:12

What Type Of Woman Am I?

Am I a single woman
With no spiritual direction
Being loose mind, body, and soul
Having no Heaven Connection Luke 7:39

Am I a widow who use to be just a wife
Having my husband head and Jesus second in my life
Psalms 146:9

Am I a divorcee feeling like I am free
Living a carnal life being all that I should not be
Matthew 5:32

Am I a married woman playing slip and slide
Running from God and my husband knowing I can not hide
Romans 7:2

OR

Am I a saved single woman
Seeking to be Jesus bride
While God prepares me
For the other side 1Corinthians 7:25

Am I a saved widow exercising righteousness
Reaping the full benefits of being deeply blessed
Proverbs 11:5

Am I a saved divorcee putting the past behind me
Knowing that Jesus will guide further than I can see
1 Timothy 4:3

Am I a saved married woman putting God first in my life
Being a spiritual mother along with being a Christian wife
Ephesians 5:22

Women ask yourselves the question —
"What type of woman am I?"

Patiently

I waite patiently Lord, for You to do a great work in me
Colossians 1:11

Further than any eyes can see 1Corinthians 2:9

Lord, I ask for food, clothes, money in my
pocket, a car to drive Matt 6:25-34

And a decent career, to keep my hopes
and dreams alive Psalms 42:5

But When God? When? Acts 1:7

I waite patiently Lord, for You to do
a great work in me 2Corinthians 6:4-10

I come to realize Lord, it's not the tangible things
that matter to You Proverbs 11:28

It's the Heavenly ordered things,
You want us to say, have, and do
Romans 9:23-26

I waite patiently Lord, for You to do a great work in me
Colossians 3:23

I come to realize Lord, You want all of your
children to possess Your Love, Your Peace,
Your Joy, and Your Happiness Galatians 5:22

While laboring as a Righteous Christian, being greatly Blessed
Matthew 5:8

I waite patiently Lord, for You to do a Great Work in Me
1Corinthians 13:4

Spoken by James, a servant of God and of the Lord Jesus Christ.

"My brethren, count it all joy when you fall into various trials, knowing that the testing of your faith produces patience. But let patience have its perfect work, that you may be perfect and complete, lacking nothing."

James 1:2-4

PSALMS 27:14

Awakening To Morning Glory

My first is my first which is my morning Glory
I present this thought as a daily true Story

It's great to awake with a mind set to adore
Jesus is with us during the sleep and the snore

So don't abuse the thought of having a good night's rest
From never ending turmoil's of every day tests

A breath of fresh air
A kneel and a prayer

Listener take heed:
Stop, think, & digest the feel of God's Glory
As you think of Jesus in this story

Knowing that it's Him and not we
Each day our eyes open to see

Psalms 25:15

The Simple Things Are Really Big

A simple Jesus loves you
to someone in distress
Could grow into a
Big Jesus Loves You
as one goes through a Spiritual Test

A simple hello could grow into a
Big Hello
to someone never spoken to
If you would stop and think ones life
could change
if you would allow Jesus to speak
through you

Catch on to exercising the simple pleasures
of *Daily Love*
While Operating Christian Behavior
sent from *Heaven Above*

1Thessalonians 1:3

GOD

When In Trouble Do Not Run From God

Run To God!

Kiss the Son, lest he be angry, and ye perish from the way,
when his wrath is kindled but a little,
Blessed are all they that put their trust in him.
Psalms 2:12

JUST TELL JESUS

There were words spoken
that should not have been said
Who shall be told?

Just Tell Jesus

There were things that were done
that should not have been done
Who shall be told?

Just Tell Jesus

The company that was kept
was not keepable company
Who shall be told?

Just Tell Jesus

The places that were visited
were not vacation sites
Who shall be told?

Just Tell Jesus

The thinking was not
justifiable thoughts
Who shall be told?

Just Tell Jesus

The secret that I long to tell
Who shall be told?

Just Tell Jesus

Psalms 32:7

There use to be an old religious hymn that was sung at a local church titled,
"Just Tell Jesus All Of Your Troubles
& He Will Never Leave You Alone."
This song placed an everlasting impression on my heart, as I matured and experienced life.

GENESIS
REVELATION

It's Written

Our Name Is Written In
The Lamb Book Of Life
And
Not Even You
Can Mess It Up!

Revelation 21:27

GOD'S CHILDREN CAN NOT BE SET UP

Life is full of war games
We fight to win but some one has to loose

The type of ammunition you use
Determines the enemy's outlook bruise

But first we must put on our armor
Loading our waist with truth

Knowing God's Children Can Not Be Set Up

Shodding the feet with preparation of peace
Shielding with faith to quench fiery darts

Knowing God's Children Can Not Be Set Up

A helmet of salvation
A sword of the spirit

Knowing God's Children Can Not Be Set Up

Praying always with prayer and supplication
Battling the war game with no vacation

Knowing God's Children Can Not Be Set UP

For God's children, it is a never ending fight
Fighting all day & praying all night

It comforts us to know
God's Children Can Not Be Set Up

Ephesians Chapter 6:11&13

WE ENTER TO FIGHT & EXIT A WINNER

We worked for many wasted years
Displaying hurt
With unconstitutional tears

We washed dishes, wiped the kids nose
And took out trash
Earning a few coins of your dirty cash

WE ENTER TO FIGHT & EXIT A WINNER

We controlled the fields to till, plow, & pluck
Hoping that a family member
Was not being used for another man's luck

WE ENTER TO FIGHT & EXIT A WINNER

Our learning ability was limited
To listening to you
Picking up nouns & verbs
To get us through

WE ENTER TO FIGHT & EXIT A WINNER

The Exit is getting closer day by day
Looking up to Jesus, there is a definite way

WE ENTER TO FIGHT & EXIT A WINNER

The Battle is not ours, it's the Lord's.

11 Corinthians 10:3-13

SURVIVAL

Field is where I go to care after and sew
because Survival Is What I Know

Wanting to be a business man
Washing education under the sand
Survival Is What I Know

Seeing mom & dad sweat at the eyebrow
Loading the mule, to ride & plow
Survival Is What I Know

A mouth of twelve or more had to be fed
Working hard to help out, with nothing said
Survival Is What I Know

Skipping school to make amends
Helping mom & dad tie loose ends
Survival Is What I Know

Sis. & Bro. may not be fully aware
James worked hard to get them there
Survival Is What I Know

Giving up school, *education* that is
So my family would comfortably live
Survival Is What I Know

They lacked for none
My parents & I worked past the sun
Survival Is What I Know

My siblings & I made it to adulthood
The world imbalanced, we never quite understood
Survival Is What I Know

LUKE 9:61

This poem is dedicated to our dad, James Edward.

SIBLINGS

Thank you God for blessing me with a brother
Thank you God for blessing me with two sisters

It is unique, the way you spaced us
Keeping the maturity level up and ceasing the fuss

Lord you placed us, as easy as one, two, three
Beginning with the oldest to little ole me

One of the girls lead the child pack
While nine months later, a boy developed in mother's sack

Later, another girl came along
Building from the others strength
To be made strong

More love took place and what did you see
Mom walking like a duck, while carrying me

We trade no one for the other
Living special as sisters & brother

Hazel, James B., & Jeanette are heart treasures.
Love Ya!

1 John 2:10

Heaven
Sent

HEAVEN SENT MOM

You are the apple of many eyes
Bearing endless fruit

The seed of many countless flowers
And the strength of many weaknesses

You are Heaven sent

You are the strongest species
Forever walking this planet

You love, You Comfort, You shape, size, & make
You care, You take, You put in, You take out,
You give & receive

During the time of time
A special or no reason at all
You are there to help lead, guide, and direct
With a sharp wing to gently protect

You are Heaven sent

Countless words could describe
What is meant

But for you, *My Dear*, there is only two
You are *"Heaven Sent"*

Matthew 15:4

This poem is dedicated to our mother, Alice Harrison.

FAMILY TREE

I thank God for our family tree
Growing up
Seeing who's a part of me

A seed of young and a breed of old
Gathering & telling stories never told

We eat for belly fulfillment
We laugh for a mind release
Only to enjoy just one day of family peace *(family reunion)*

The family tree is designed to be a mass of love
Sent from God's Son
Who is sitting above

He knew when He created our huge Oak Tree
What it would be
While including you & me

He also knew down this family line
With special creations
His makings took time

An Aint here
An uncle there
As we grew older
Family was found everywhere

Our family is rich with many breeds
Going back to the root
Of only One True Family Seed

Thinking of the Harrison and Sumner / Vines family.
The seeds from which my parents were formed.

1st John 3:9

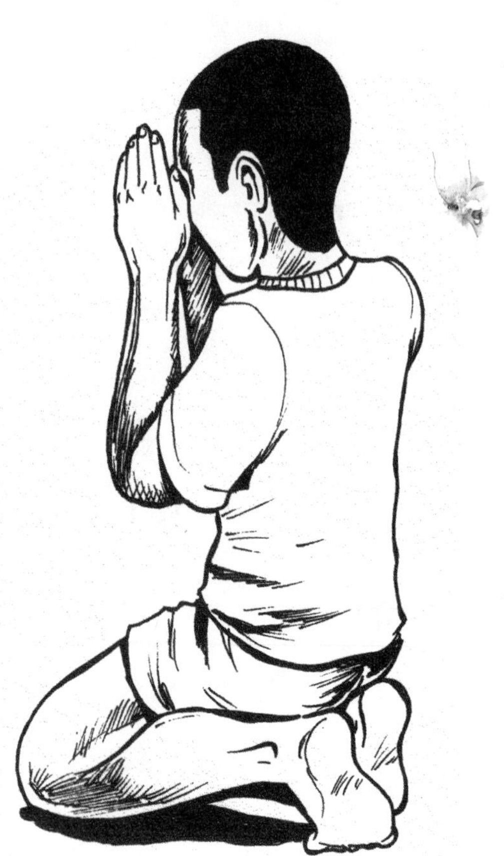

Only When We Pray

We are helpless
Sure Help Is On The Way
Only When We Pray

We have fallen from the tallest tree
Sure Help Is On The Way
Only When We Pray

Our mistakes were made for the correction
Sure Help Is On The Way
Only When We Pray

The job failed
Sure Help Is On The Way
Only When We Pray

The possessions we had went up for sale
Sure Help Is On The Way
Only When We Pray

We feel like a group of zombies prone for jail
Sure Help Is On The Way
Only When We Pray

We fight off the enemy with the strongest arm
Sure Help Is On The Way
Only When We Pray

Luke 18:1 - 8

FAITH

Believe God

Receive His Words

Maintain Faith

Hebrews 4:14

PROTECT MY INNOCENT SOUL

Dear Heavenly Father:

It's your child again, coming to receive the protection for my innocent soul. Jesus, my enemies desire to sift me like wheat. Luke 22:31-32 But You have prayed for me. Romans 8:27 Sometimes I get so helpless in natural strength, while viewing the weakness of the enemy. But You have made it known unto man, that the enemies occupation is destruction. Knowing that he is envy for the cause and she is jealous for the effect. They try to hide but the enemy's wickedness is written all over them, starting at head and ending at feet. Their weakness display signs of, "I want, I want, I want. I want her looks, I want her job, I want her family, I want her dead or alive." But important enough, I want who lives inside of her, *Jesus.*

Why do people birth evil seeds? Do they lack Truth in their lives? Could it be the hair style, the attire on my back, a couple of earned graduation rings? Jesus, all of these things are temporal. The appearance of the flesh, with material possessions are all seconds away, from being called the past. I've thought about my education stamina, my career, my boldness in You, my mother wick, the pep in my step, the look, the attitude, the ore, that makes the enemy lurk to destroy, what You created. The enemy has problems with people for many unjustifiable excuses. For there is no true reason for enemy behavior. They carry false accusations. When You died on the cross and rose the third day, with all power in Your Hands, You made available the tree of life for everyone. Rev. 22:14

But I come to realize, from all the things mentioned, the enemy hated You for Righteousness sake. Paul did say, "And even as they did not like to retain God in their knowledge,

God gave them over to a debased mind, to do those things which are not fitting. Romans 1:28

Becoming Your child and obeying Your word, I am envied for my boldness in You, my soul worth, my understanding, my speaking, and teaching of Your word. None being less, Your word says in the book of James 4:7, "Resist the devil and he will flee from you." David stated, "He guards the paths of the justice, And preserves the way of His saints. Psalms 2:8

For Your word, Jesus, is Based on Truth for a righteous man and woman to Obey. Through all the idols that has the enemy distracted, protect my innocent soul from the evil one. Prov 2:8

Father, with Your Protection, my soul finds rest.
You are my Hedge of Protection.

STABLE FEET

If we don't stay prayed up, as we all need to
The enemy will attempt to walk, talk, and run all over you

When we are rooted from the Off Spring of the
Most High King
We have the Authority to make the enemy scream

How can I kill, steal, and destroy? *the enemy may say*
Jesus response, You are defeated when my children pray

Christians, take charge of the enemy, while in defeat
By holding Spiritual Anchor, with stable feet

Hebrew 6:19

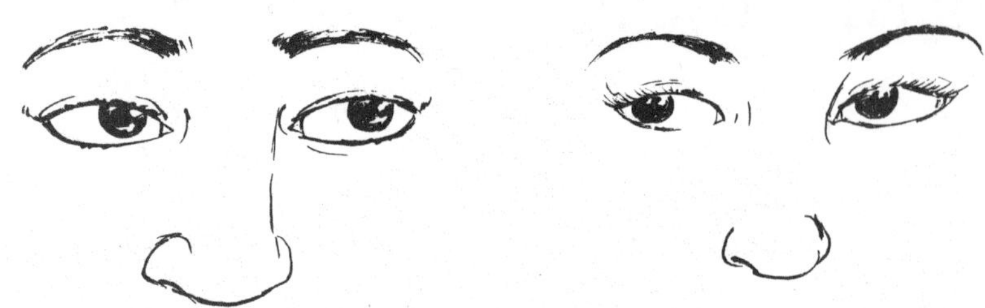

WATCH

If You Watch Your Friends

Your Enemies

Will Be Harmless

Matthew 26:41

PEACE BE STILL ENEMY

I know you target and try to destroy
Because you discovered our Maker did not create a toy
Proverbs 11:9

Peace Be Still Enemy

From our personal to public life
Enemy you've tried to create misery and strife Luke 10:19

Peace Be Still Enemy

You've tried to plant, the demonic seed of death
While tampering with family and personal health Psalms 23:4

Peace Be Still Enemy

Enemy you come to tear up more than our homes and health
By snatching God's word and our Ordained Wealth
Deuteronomy 8:18

I say to you again, Peace Be Still Enemy

We see you looking as you try to hide
While wondering if Jesus is really on our side Romans 8:1

Peace Be Still Enemy

Enemy your character is worse than any presented dream
But your job is to be envious, jealous, and spitefully mean
Galatians 5:18-21

Peace Be Still Enemy

Enemy, you try to come in a secret disguise
Not speaking the truth but many lies 1John 2:21

Peace Be Still Enemy

Get scared because we saints are out to destroy you
For all the filth you put us through Isaiah 4:4

Enemy I extend my words only to say

Darkness can never shine when it is day Genesis 1:4

Your time is just about up
God's people are tired of you passing your bitter cup
Hosea 10:12

Peace Be Still Enemy 1King 5:4

FORGIVENESS

Forgiveness Is Provided Like The Fresh Air We Breathe

Psalms 30

Gift Certificate
Chocolates
BIBLE

LOVE SYNERGY

Love Leads

Love Guides

Love Directs

Love Corrects

Love Connects

Love Uplifts

Love Sparks

Love Vibrates

Love Sanctify

Love Justify

Love Loves

Jude 1:1&2

JESUS THE COVENANT KEEPER

Dear Jesus:

Your child has come in prayer. As I continue my Holy walk with You, I am reminded of the Covenant that You had with Noah and how he was a just man. He walked upright in Your presence. You were so kind, as to establish a Covenant with Noah's descendants. *Gen 9:9*

Jesus, You instructed Moses to tell the children of Israel, "You have seen with your own eyes what I did to the Egyptians, and how I bore you on eagles' wings and brought you to Myself. Now if you will indeed obey My voice and keep my Covenant, then you shall be a special treasure to Me above all people; for all the earth is Mine." *Exo 19:14*

As you instituted the Lord's Supper, You took the wine and said, "This is My blood of the New Covenant, which is shed for many." After supper, You took the cup and said, "This cup is the New Covenant in My blood, which is shed for you. But behold, the hand of My betrayer is with Me on the table. *Luk 22:20*

I am instantly reminded of Jerusalem and how you dealt with them and their wrong doings. Your words through Ezekiel to Jerusalem, "I will deal with you as you have done, who despised the oath by breaking the covenant. Nevertheless I will remember My covenant with you in the days of your youth, and I will establish an everlasting covenant with you. Then you will remember your ways and be ashamed, when you receive your older and your younger sisters; for I will give them to you for daughters, but not because of My covenant with you. And I will establish My covenant with you. Then you shall know that I am the Lord, that you may remember and be ashamed, and never open your mouth anymore because of your shame, when I provide you an atonement for all you have done." Ezekiel

Like many of Your people, who You placed a Covenant with, betrayed You. We went back on our promises, by performing some type of sinful act; causing the full potential of the Covenant on our behalf, to fall short. Jesus, because You are a Man of Your word and can not lie, You remain the Covenant Keeper for Your chosen vessels. *Num 23:19-20*
Jesus, continue to hold steady to the assembly line of my daily operation, as a Holy woman, knowing that You will always be my Covenant Keeper.

This is my prayer unto You, Jesus.

COVERED

Everyday Of My Life
Is Being
Covered Under
The Blood
Of
Jesus!

Romans 4:7

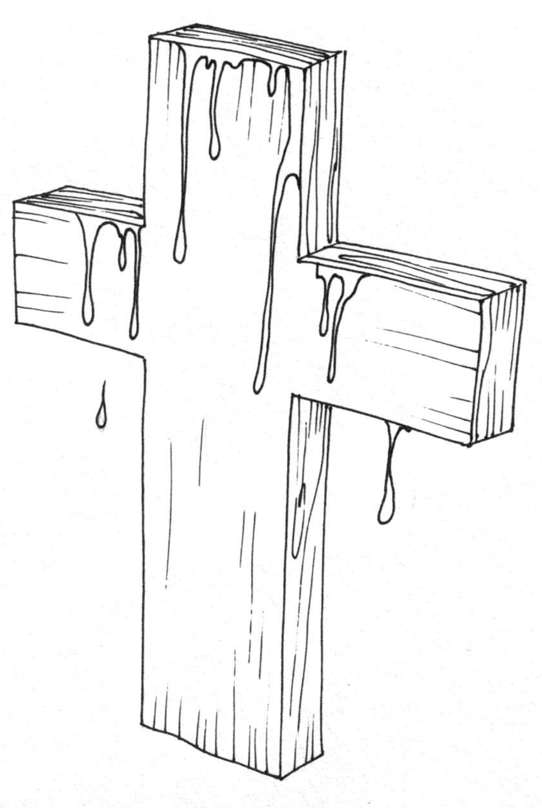

THE BLOOD

Israel, Oh! Israel!
The animal blood protected your family & health
While putting up with Egypt & their deceitful self

The Blood Israel! The Blood! The Blood!

Israel you didn't have enough faith, to receive blood protection
But God found favor to show affection

The Blood Israel! The Blood! The Blood!

Israel, the God we serve got tired of you
He giving orders and you doing what you want to do

The Blood Israel! The Blood! The Blood!

God patients with you became a thin line
The only thing that helped, was God & Moses communication time

The Blood Israel! The Blood! The Blood!

A difference came about, from your generation to mine
We are served with blood, of the Most High Divine

The Blood Israel! The Blood! The Blood!

Understand, the Blood washes away sins of all mankind
Once the Cleanse, Purity you will find

The Blood Israel! The Blood! The Blood!

Jesus Blood shed was God's decision
Giving up His son & making provision

The Blood! The Blood! The Blood!

Hebrews 9:18 - 22

Cousin William Harrison, Jr., this poem is dedicated to you.

LOVE GOT TO DO WITH IT

You call us insane
When we show you sanctification

Love Got To Do With It

You spit at us
When we blow you a kiss

Love Got To Do With It

You threaten to kill
When we prove ourselves to live

Love Got To Do With It

You play with our mind
As we display genuine heart signs

Love Got To Do With It

Many really don't know
It takes God to make love show

Love Got To Do With It

Numbers 14:18-23

devil With A Problem

Upset with us for our Spiritual Cover?
While mirroring self, you saw the other

devil with a problem

Is it when we walk, we step tall
Being God's child, who's got it all

God showed us what life really could be
As we're obedient, the full view is to see

devil with a problem

You may have seen us up & now it seems we are down
But we're looking up to Jesus & not around

Stop focusing on our development levels in life
Hurting yourself with ungodly strife

devil with a problem

Clean up self and make positive things happen to
Stop living in darkness, with others thinking identical to you

Our life was predestined by God's choice

Holy One, let's give the devil no opportunity for voice

Galatians 5:26

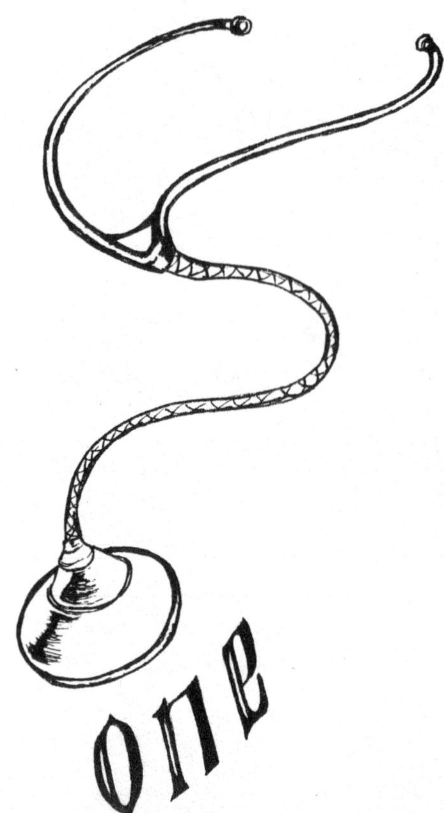
one

THERE'S ONLY ONE TRUE DOCTOR

He healed the sick
He raised the dead
Five thousand souls, He willfully fed

There's Only One True Doctor

He's not a practitioner
He's not a specialist

There's only one Name for Him THE BEST

There's Only One True Doctor

God's arm can reach the deepest womb
His finger can heal the most tender spot

There's Only One True Doctor

He's a doctor of truth
Not a physician full of lies

There's Only One True Doctor

He treat the cause of the problem
Not the symptoms

There's Only One True Doctor

Before you seek a practicing physician
Have a talk with the Only One True Doctor

Matthew 10:8

GOD
PAIN
PEACE

INGREDIENTS FOR BECOMING A FULL TIME VET

1	Dose	of the big picture
1	Pinch	of pain
1	Cup	of understanding with more to gain
50	Gallons	of distilled faith
		For the hidden findings
7	Ounces	of experienced knowledge
		without the need of college
12	packages	of patients
20	quarts	of peace
		For God to provide a complete recipe
		An
8	speed	Blender is required to mix the mix
		To give the veteran a full time fix
100	Percent	Full Time Vet Ingredient

This poem is dedicated to all of the retired citizens, who have worked honest and hard at what they possess.
Love, Peace, & Happiness be unto you all.

Ephesians 4:1& 2

I AM THAT I AM

I demanded the demons
To exit Legion St. Mark 5:8

I spoke and commanded
Lazarus grave clothes to be loosed St. John 11:44

I Am That I Am

The king found favor
In Queen Esther Esther 8:5

On the day of Pentecost
The Holy Ghost surely came Acts 2:1

Paul was converted
On the road to Damascus Acts 9:3

I Am That I Am

I instructed Moses
To lead the children of Israel Exodus 3:11 &12

I kept Peter from sinking
Just like I opened the red sea Exodus 15:4

I AM THAT I AM

David knew Who gave him the talent
As a mighty musician Psalms 147:7

Matthew knew where his
Tax collecting skills Birthed Matthew 11:19

I Am That I Am

I give unto you power to tread on
serpents and scorpions and over all
the power of the enemy St. Luke 10:19

Always Remember
When Jesus, the "I Am That I Am" speaks
Everyone and everything must listen St. Luke 3:14

Acts 16:31

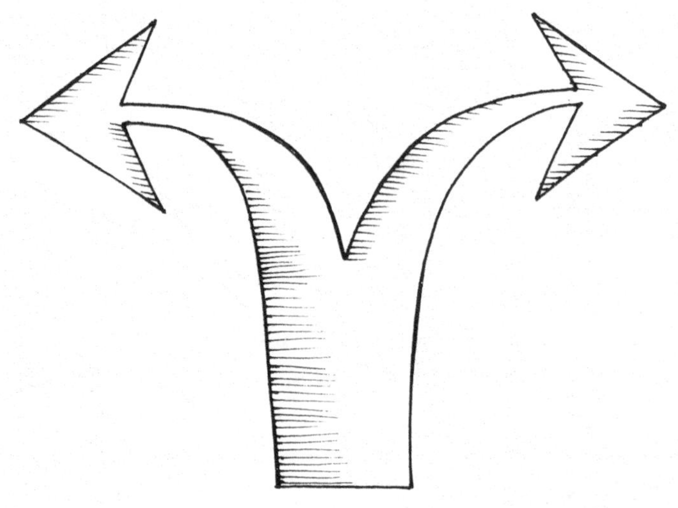

RIGHT

If I Can't Do It Right
I Refuse To Do It Wrong

1st King 15:4&5

SOUL SEARCHING

Every time we get slack on the job
Jesus pick & pull at our hearts knob

We are soul searching
The True Christian That Is

Striving to keep righteous steps in our walk
Raising the antenna of our body & vocal talk

We are soul searching
The True Christian That Is

Before winning a soul
First, ours must be searched

Allowing Jesus to tear down only to rebuild
Repairing and replacing for the Golden Seal

We are soul searching
The True Christian That is

Once the repair and replacements are complete
A sinner's soul, we can continue to seek

We are soul searching
The True Christian That Is

Ezekiel 18:4

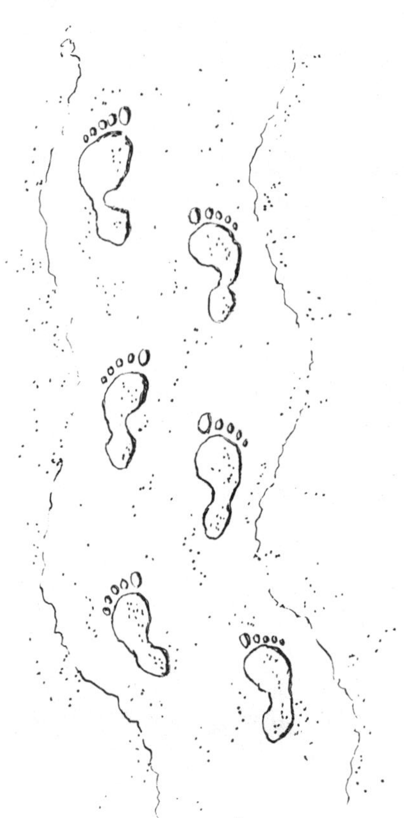

WALKING IN MY PURPOSE

Dear Jesus:

I have come to place a prayer at the Throne of Grace. I've heard You, Jesus; the call, the choosing, the elect, the one, among many members.

Jesus, I have heard Your voice and I take heed to Your orders, but I need You, Jesus, to forever be with me.

Before I even get started with Your work, the enemy wishes to tear it down. But Your Holy Word says, "Do not fret because of evildoer's, nor be envious of the worker's of iniquity. For they shall soon be cut down like the grass, and wither as the green herbs." *Psalms 37:1-2*

So the Discerning Spirit from within will be watchful for these unrighteous acts of the enemy, as I remain steadfast and immovable in You. I am forewarned in Your word to be mindful. *Hebrew 2:6-9*

You have made me aware of quite a few important things, while walking in Your purpose. I will travel beside counterfeits; hear words go forth out of the mouths of false prophets; see powerless laying on of hands, as people are cursed instead of blessed; acknowledge tithes being paid to wolves displayed in white collars and robes, as they trample in sheep clothing. Proverbs 14:5

Dear Jesus, Your Shield of Protection will guide me, when a smile comes to my face and a knife awaits my back. As the killer weapons are aimed, it is imperative to stand on Genesis to Revelation, knowing Your word Overpowers the powerless.

Blessed assurance has come from Your dedicated servant Paul, who was appointed to apostleship. He made it known to the Galatians of it being only one gospel. He said to the people, "I marvel that you are turning away so soon from Him who called you in the grace of Christ, to a different gospel, which is not another but there are some who trouble you and want to pervert the gospel of Christ." Galatians 1:6-7 Paul continued in the same passages of scripture by saying, "For do I now persuade men, or God? Or do I seek to please men? For if I still pleased men, I would not be a servant of God. For I neither received it from man, nor was I taught it, but it came through revelation of Jesus Christ." Galatians 1:10&12

All of these things, I take into account, for many are called to perform a work for You, while few are chosen. *Matthew 22:14 / 24:4-14*

Jesus, teach me to carry out Your leadership duties according to Your will and Your way.

Psalms 46:10

DON'T TAKE IT PERSONAL

Single Christian women seek to be sin free
With our eyes on the prize of perfection

DON'T TAKE IT PERSONAL

Faced with fleshly torment of intimate provokes
We seek after victory deliverance

DON'T TAKE IT PERSONAL

There are Holy demands placed in our lives
As we focus on the Everlasting Life, that only Jesus offers

DON'T TAKE IT PERSONAL

Wondering why our disposition appears strange
It must be displayed, we are in a Distinctive Army

DON'T TAKE IT PERSONAL

Our eyes are clear
And our lips are clean
Making the appearance
While being the example, of a Christian Queen

DON'T TAKE IT PERSONAL

Acts 11:26

Dedicated to all single women who are Living Holy.

GLORY

Don't Get Confused With Who Gets The Glory!

Jesus

ALPHA & OMEGA
THE BEGINNING & THE ENDING
THE FIRST & THE LAST
EL-Shaddai
JEHOVAH-jireh
JEHOVAH-rophe
JEHOVAH-nissi
JEHOVAH-M'Kaddesh

JEHOVAH-shalom
JEHOVAH-tsidkenu
JEHOVAH-rohi
JEHOVAH-shammah
THE STONE ***the builder's rejected***
THE KING
I AM
WONDERFUL
GREAT
Lord the Father

Isaiah 42:8

Returning To Our Maker

The body will return back to dust
As the revealing casket turns to rust

This might sound horrible to the natural ear
But those of the spirit are listening to hear

Keep in mind, it's not as bad as it may seem
God appointed another, to complete his T.E.A.M.

We are not out roaming all alone
Understand the body is dust & the souls at home

Everyone's day is coming to meet the maker
When you are Saved
There is no such thing as the undertaker

This is a sentimental piece that is designed to comfort those who feel like they have lost a love one, when only the deceased has gone away to spiritually meet the Creator. This is dedicated to all the family with deceased loved ones, who have lived a Christian life and it showed among mankind.

Ecclesiastes 7:2

BIBLE

ELDERLY BLESSINGS

Dear Jesus:

I come with a prayer for Your Blessings to be sent to the elderly. Many of them are living with total acknowledgment of Your outstretched arms. Never forgetting David's sealed words, "I have been young, and now I am old; Yet I have never seen the righteous forsaken, nor His descendants begging bread. He is ever merciful, and lends; And His descendants are Blessed." *Psalms 37:25-26*

The elderly memories of years past mistreatment, fleshly defeats, and torments are remembered but because of their strong anchor in faith, Your grace and mercy has supplied them with the power to depend on You and only You. During Peter's message to the pilgrims, he spoke, "The elders who are among you, I exhort, I who am a fellow elder and a witness of the sufferings of Christ, and also a partaker of the glory that will be revealed: Shepherd the flock of God which is among you, serving as overseers, not by constraint but willingly, not for dishonest gain but eagerly; you, but being examples to the flock; and when the Chief Shepherd appears, you will receive the crown of glory that does not fade away." 1Peter 5:1-4

As elder spiritual lectures are presented to new generations, I can imagine them saying these words, being passed on from Paul, "When I was a child, I spoke as a child, I understood as a child, I thought as a child; but when I became a man, I put away childish things. 1Cor 13:11

As I represent this prayer as a Holy woman, I ask in Your name, Jesus, to continue to multiply years of life to their existence, demanding the world to place them at Honor's Door.

For Your word says, "Let the elders who rule be counted worthy of double honor, especially those who labor in the word and doctrine. 1 Tim 5:17
Their youth has designed a cut path, for the old age to be their "Golden Days." I continuously pray that Your blessings, *Dear Jesus,* will compass their way.

Hang in there grandpa Sylvester. Your 80 plus years of life is a Heavenly Blessing!

THREE SCORE AND TEN

I have seen the lightning flash
I have heard thunder roar
3 & 10 is my score

Time brought
happy
sad
disappointments
appointments
put ups
let downs
But this little stuff did not stop me
For my life was built on a Spiritual History

It is true
I have seen a lot of passed years
With smiling faces and watered tears

One important thing that I must say
Never forget to stop and Pray

As you obey God, while free from sin
You will be given 3 score 10

This poem is dedicated to the elderly, who still lives obedience unto Christ. Thank you for the backbone grip.
Young and middle age folk, take heed to this message.

Genesis 6

We are guaranteed 120 years or longer.

AWARENESS

Don't Mistake A HELPING HAND For A Grenade Cap

Isaiah 65:2

IMPOSSIBLE

Making Sense Of Evil
Is
A DEFINITE
IMPOSSIBLE!

I will early destroy all the wicked of the land; that I may cut off all wicked doers from the city of the Lord.

Psalms 101:8

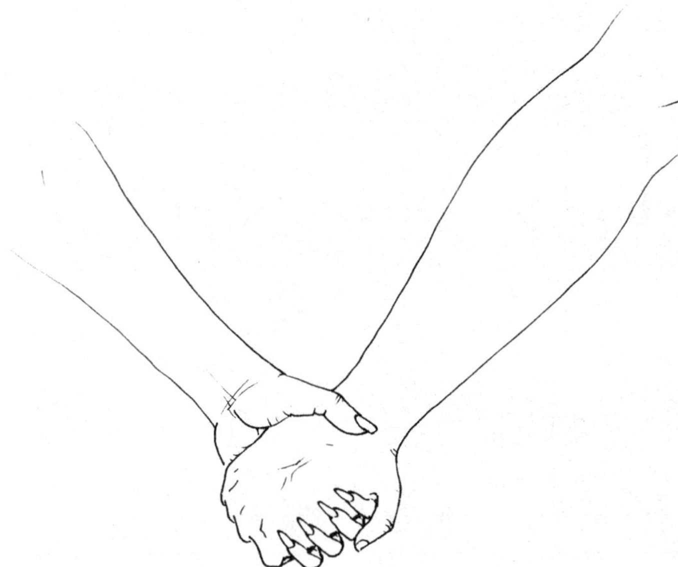

HAND IN HAND

Your hand
My hand
A connection

The permanent attachment
For the slip of a finger

A path
A way in
A way out
Hand in Hand

We connect for the Love
Peace
Joy
Direction
Placing a bond on the never ending
Connection
Hand in Hand

Leaning
Trusting
Depending
While Thanking God for the upper sending

Self Evident
You are the *Man*
Walking with Your people
Hand in Hand

1 Timothy 2:8

This poem is dedicated to cousin Francis Perry. Her encouraging words to me were "Just Keep Your Hand In Gods Hand."

LET GOD BE GOD

Speaking into Existence
Building Up
Tearing Down
Repairing to Make
Molding to Shape

Let God Be God

Instructing
Alerting
Baptizing
Converting

Let God Be God

Calling
Choosing
Anointing
Appointing

Let God Be God

Birthing

Giving

Taking

Receiving

Let God Be God

No one can touch the operation of God, through His Son Jesus.

John 1

THE POWER OF LOVE

The Power of Love. . . . . Is deeper than it's actual spelling

Hate & Hurt are not included

The Power of Love. . . . . Is deep in feeling & vibrates for the showing

Love can be Said

Love can be Silent

Love can be Felt

The Power Of Love . . . . Operates like a measuring scale, only for the Spiritual Balance

You mean what you Say
And perform Love Actions Everyday

The Power Of Love Continues

When you hurt, I hurt
When you are up, I am up
When you need, I will provide
I will be strong, when you are weak

The Power Of Love . . . . Stops an argument before it starts
Controls the finances
Disciplines the children
Brings reasoning within reasoning

By Allowing Jesus to be the Power in your Love
Will sanctify the marriage, sent directly from Heaven above

The Power Of Love

Ephesians 5:22

This was a poem specifically created for my sister, Jeanette on her special day, June 19, 1999. May Heaven smile upon you and your family.

CURSED FOR THE BLESSING

Going unnoticed
The owl
The witch
The full moon
The secret concoction
Grave yard dirt
String of hair
Picture
Clock
Collection
Developed from an envy obsession

Cursed For The Blessing

God's Spiritual Alert comes upon us
The inner gut of attention
Why all the death threats

You
Your thoughts
Your beliefs
Your practices
Your soul
Selling yourself to the devil
Going to hell
If you don't make a change

Cursed For The Blessing

Setting us up for a deadly trap
Exploding in your presence

Lights out
The rabbits foot
The monkey's ear
The skeletal remains
The crystal ball

All gone up in smoke
As the curse turns into a Blessing

Nehemiah 13:2
To all of the false saints, fake friends, and real enemies, who try so hard to take a good man or woman down, Understand God at His Word. He will Bless those who Bless, and Curse those who Curse.

GIFTED

God'S Children Are Multi-Talented

Skilled For The Skill

Every good and perfect gift is from above, and cometh down from the Father of lights, with whom is no variableness, neither shadow of turning.

James 1:17

CUT FOR THE FITTING

Dark
Dirty
Object
It's Hidden

My Value
My Worth
Resting in a Mine

Existing for the Appearance

Using not a Saw nor a Drill

Chip by Chip
Scrape by Scrape
Carve by Carve
Leaving No Remains

Design by Design
Cut for the Fitting

A Diamond is a Precious Jewel.

First Lady Jesse Alston, Thank You for the revelation, that was given to me on our way to New York in 1997. You used a "Diamond," for an example, of how God was creating my Spiritual Walk. As you read, I have created a poem from the key word that you used, "Diamond."

John 15

A BURDEN FOR THE BURDEN BEARER

Dear Jesus:

I have come to You with this weight. It is so heavy, I can hardly walk, from the pressure on my spine. My ears are overloaded with these untamed sounds. My eyes are bleared, from what is seen in the flesh. My mind is drenched with this unfamiliar speech of agony. The synergy is like a cave without an exit.

Finding the image of what appears to be a door, I grip the handle. I don't need help, the strength is there for the tightening. So I hold on hoping to see light. As the grip loosened through the sweaty palm of my right hand, I switch to the left. The knob slipped away.

As I continue to bow my head & talk with You; I am remaining at Your throne of grace & mercy, for You to take my burdens. Without a shadow of a doubt, *You are my Burden Bearer*. When I tried to operate from my personal strength, the burden's weight lowered me into this caves quick sand. But when my mind caught balance with my Spirit Man, Your Supernatural Power released all charges against me.

After having spoken these words, I will take Your yoke & learn of You, for You are Gentle & Lowly in heart. I will find rest for my soul. *Matt 11:29&30*

Jesus, You said, "For My yoke is easy & My burden is light."
Matt 11:30

Jesus, My Burden Bearer

Jesus Knows And This Is What Matters

Everyone has a day and this one included me
We never know when death will knock, for this we can not see

You did not know my relationship with Jesus
Except by what you saw
My soul could have left, without a sinful flaw

This is something that you will never know
Seek Jesus for yourself and be qualified to go

Matthew 19:30

To the saved and unsaved who like to judge during bereavement, God is the only judge when the final call is made.

James 4:12

This was written to fit the moment of bereavement of the late Uncle George.

WHAT'S THE MESSAGE?

Word is bond
Word with song
Word in action
Word with reaction

What could possibly be the message?

Drummer's drumming
Sachets being played
Keyboard's roaring
Words are flowing

What could possibly be the message?

Prayer prayed
Scripture read
Dialogue recited
Sermon addressed

What could possibly be the message?

Clock punched
Work day began
Laboring til hours end

What could possibly be the message?

Repeated Routine
Is It Six?
Is It Seven?
Day after Day

What Could Possibly Be The Message?

Deuteronomy 5:14-22 / Ephesians 2:9&10 /Colossians 4:1

SPIRITUAL EDUCATION

GOD LESSONS
ALL
OF US

DIFFERENT

TO REST
ON
ONE ACCORD

Ephesians 4:13&14

PRESSING BECAUSE OF MY WEAKNESSES

Dear Jesus:

I "press because of my weaknesses." I know that in You lie my very strength. As I grow older and experience life, Your word becomes more clearer, as I keep my head in what You said. Learning that obedience is better than sacrifice. *Romans 1:5&6* I still ponder over the fact that if I perform everything exact or to the "T," will obstacles still present themselves? Your word tells me that you did not come to bring peace but a sword *Matthew 10:34*, and that I may have life and have it more abundantly. Well, again Jesus, I "press because of my weaknesses."

The more I make reference to the biblical family, I come to understand, many of them pressed because of their weaknesses. I am reminded of Moses, as being lead by One of the most mighty leaders in all biblical history. He was instructed by *You*, to speak to the children of Israel, who were in bondage. Exodus 4:15-17

Because Moses was new to this assignment, he thought that his limited speaking skills were unfit for Your in depth cause. Moses spoke, "O my Lord, I am not eloquent, neither before nor since You have spoken to Your servant; but I am slow of speech and slow of tongue." Exodus 4:10

Dear Jesus, from Moses response, You asked him a few questions, "Who has made man's mouth? Or who makes the mute, the deaf, the seeing, or the blind? Have not I, the Lord? Now therefore, go, and I will be with your mouth and teach you what you shall say." Exodus 4:11-12

The Holy Word states that, Aaron, Moses brother was sent with him to be a mouth piece. You spoke words to Moses about the Israelites. He transferred the messages to Aaron. While Aaron spoke to the children of Israel, through You, Jesus, the miracles came forth from the hands of Moses. Exodus 4:14

When Isaiah was called to be a prophet, he said: “Woe is me, for I am undone! Because I am a man of unclean lips, and I dwell in the midst of a people of unclean lips; for my eyes have seen the King, the Lord of hosts.” Isaiah 6:5

These two biblical references alone helps me to press because of my weaknesses. Suffering endure for a night, and joy cometh in the morning. Psalms 30:5 As I press because of my weakness, I have rest assurance that my assigned angels are present, for my security. Luke 4:10-11

Thank you Dear Jesus for Your Supernatural Power,
for I will continue to Press Because Of My Weaknesses.
Philippines 3:14.

Philippians 3:13-16

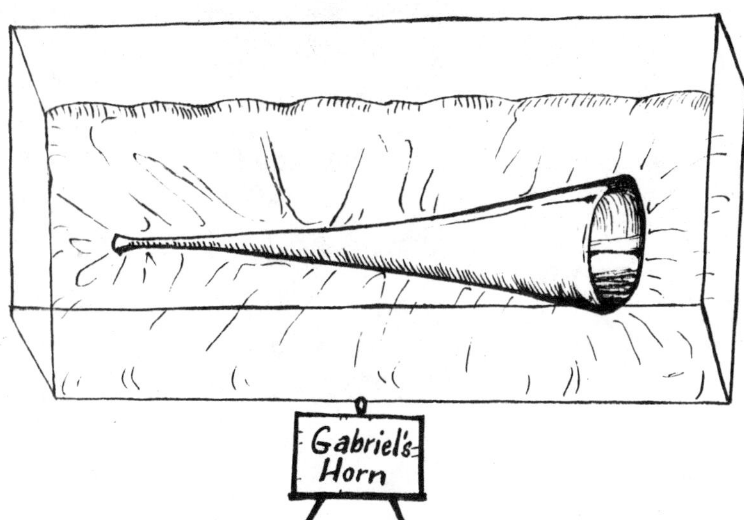
Gabriel's
Horn

Gabriel's Horn

Gabriel
Has Not Blown His
Horn
Yet
With Short Time
At Hand

Let's Get Busy For
God!

1 Thessalonians 4:16 & 18

THANK YOU AND MAY GOD CONTINUE TO BLESS YOU REAL GOOD!

JESUS WILL NOT WITHOLD NO GOOD THING FROM THE RIGHTEOUS.

PSALMS 84:11

HOLY SATISFACTION GUARANTEED!